Commercial Real Estate

Commercial Real Estate

HOW TO INVEST IN COMMERCIAL REAL ESTATE

Unlocking the Secrets of Commercial Real Estate Investing: A Comprehensive Guide to Building Wealth, Achieving Success, and Navigating the Complexities of the Commercial Property Market.

By

Gary Norton

Commercial Real Estate

DISCLAIMER

The information provided in this book is for educational and informational purposes only. While every effort has been made to ensure the accuracy and completeness of the content, the author makes no representations or warranties of any kind, express or implied, about the completeness, accuracy, reliability, suitability, or availability with respect to the information contained herein.

Any reliance you place on such information is strictly at your own risk. The author will not be liable for any losses, injuries, or damages from the display or use of this information.

The views and opinions expressed in this book are those of the author and do not necessarily reflect the official policy or position of any organization or entity.

Copyright © [2024] [Gary Norton]

About this book

In this complete reference to commercial real estate investment, we hope to offer you with the knowledge and tools you need to confusing to diversify your portfolio or a novice to the world of real estate investing, this book is intended to be your go-to reference for learning the principles, methods, and best practices of commercial real estate investment.

What you may expect to find in this book:

Insights into Commercial Real Estate: We'll begin by defining commercial real estate and discussing the numerous sorts of properties that fit into this category. You'll have a better grasp of the various asset classes, market dynamics, and investing opportunities that exist in the commercial real estate market.

Benefits and Risks of Commercial Real Estate Investment: Next, we'll look at the benefits and drawbacks of investing in commercial buildings. From high rental yields and tax breaks to vacancy concerns and market swings, we'll look at the elements that might affect your investment returns and how to minimize them efficiently.

Strategies for Success: We'll show you how to locate, evaluate, and acquire lucrative commercial real estate assets. Whether you're looking for office buildings, retail centers, industrial warehouses, or multifamily complexes, we'll provide you with the resources and information you need to make sound investment decisions.

Legal and Financial Considerations: We'll go over the legal and financial elements of commercial real estate investing, including Financing possibilities, due diligence procedures, and legal documents. You'll learn how to negotiate complicated legal systems, get funding, and undertake detailed property studies to guarantee your investments succeed.

Property Management and Optimization: Finally, we'll look at property management best practices, tenant relations, and ideas for increasing the value of your commercial properties. Whether you're a hands-on investor or prefer to outsource property management, we'll provide you professional suggestions and guidance on how to maximize your investment profits.

This book includes real-life examples, case studies, and practical advice from experienced investors and industry leaders. Whether you want to develop wealth through passive income or attain financial independence through real estate investment, this book will serve as your entire roadmap to success in the competitive world of commercial real estate.

Let us go on this trip together and discover the profitable prospects that exist in the world of commercial property investing!

TABLE OF CONTENTS

Introduction
    Why Invest in Commercial Real Estate?

Chapter 1
    Definition of a Commercial Investor
    Types of Commercial Property
    Office Building
    Retail center
    Industrial warehouse
    Multifamily apartments
    Hotels and Hospitality Properties:
    Medical and Healthcare Facilities:
    Mixed-Use Developments:

Chapter 2
    Understanding Commercial Real Estate Investing
    Advantages of Investing in Commercial Real Estate:
    Risk and Challenges:
    Factors Affecting the Commercial Real Estate Market:

Chapter 3
    An Intensive Course on Investing in Commercial Real Estate
    Recognizing the Fundamentals:
    Market Dynamics and Trends:

Investment tactics and techniques:
Due Diligence and Risk Management:
Capital Structures and Financing:
Legal and Regulatory Considerations:

Chapter 4
Getting Investment Leads for Commercial Property
Market research and analysis:
Networking and Relationship Building
Real Estate Agents and Brokers
Online Platforms and markets
Direct Marketing and Outreach
Investment Groups and Syndicates

Chapter 5
Commercial Deal Negotiation and Closure
Comprehending the Process of Negotiation
Communication
Negotiation Dynamics
Resolution of disputes
Handling the Process of Due Diligence
Property Inspection
Legal & Regulatory conformity
Tenant Analysis
Essential Facts to Take Into Account When Sealing Commercial Deals
Executing legal Documents
Funding and Financing
Ownership Examination and Insurance

Closing monies and Escrow
Title Transfer and Recording

Chapter 6
    Overseeing and Regulating Business Real Estate
    Top Property Management Techniques
    Financial Management:
    Tenant Selection and Screening
    Property Inspections and Maintenance
    Risk Management and Compliance
    Important factors for lease agreements and tenant relations
    Effective Communication
    Lease negotiation
    Tenant Services and Amenities
    Tenant Retention tactics
    Strategies for Upkeep and Maintenance
    Scheduled Inspections
    Emergency Response Planning
    Capital Improvement Projects
    Risk mitigation and Return Optimization
    Techniques for Risk Management
    Exercise Due Diligence
    Risk Assessment
    Monitoring and Adaptation

Chapter 7
    The Management of Portfolios and Diversification

Important facets of portfolio management and diversification
Asset Allocation
Risk Management instrument
Techniques to Raise the Value of Your Property
Capital improvements
Operational Efficiency
Success Stories and Real-Life Case Studies
Case Studies of Profitable Investments in Commercial Real Estate:
Redevelopment of Office Buildings
Retail mall Repositioning
Expansion of an Industrial Warehouse
Principal Learning Outcomes and Conclusions:
Planning and Strategic Vision
The Tenant-Centric Approach
Flexibility and Adaptability

Chapter 8
Your Next Moves in Investing in Commercial Real Estate
Formulating Your Investment Strategy
Establish Your Investment Goals
Evaluate Your Risk Profile
Establish Investment criterion
Create a Diversified Portfolio Strategy
Establish an Actionable Investment Plan
Further Reading Materials & Resources:

Supplementary Materials and Index

Commercial Real Estate

Sites and Organizations Suggested
Glossary of Terms Used in Commercial Real Estate:
Last Thought

Commercial Real Estate

Introduction

Welcome to the exciting world of commercial real estate investing! In this book, we will embark on a journey to explore the ins and outs of investing in commercial properties, uncovering the opportunities and potential pitfalls that come with this dynamic market.

Commercial real estate investing offers a unique set of benefits and challenges, making it an attractive option for savvy investors looking to diversify their portfolios and generate passive income streams. From office buildings and retail spaces to industrial warehouses and multifamily complexes, commercial properties encompass a wide range of asset classes with varying risk profiles and potential returns.

But what exactly is commercial real estate, and why should you consider investing in it? In the following chapters, we will delve into the definition of commercial real estate, discussing the different types of properties and the characteristics of commercial investors.

We will also explore the myriad benefits of commercial real estate investing, from lucrative rental yields and tax advantages to portfolio diversification and long-term wealth accumulation.

However, investing in commercial real estate is not without its challenges. From navigating complex legal and regulatory frameworks to conducting thorough due diligence and property analysis, there are numerous factors to consider before making an investment decision. Throughout this book, we will provide you with practical insights, strategies, and best practices to help you navigate these challenges and make informed investment choices.

Whether you are a seasoned investor looking to expand your portfolio or a newcomer to the world of real estate investing, this book is designed to equip you with the knowledge, tools, and confidence you need to succeed in the competitive world of commercial real estate. So, let's dive in and discover the wealth-building opportunities that await in the realm of commercial property investing!

But what exactly is commercial real estate, and why should you invest in it? In the next chapters, we will define commercial real estate, review the various types of properties, and examine the characteristics of commercial investors. We will also look at the many advantages of investing in commercial real estate, such as high rental yields and tax breaks, as well as portfolio diversification and long-term wealth growth.

However, investing in commercial real estate presents its own set of obstacles. Before making an investment choice, various issues must be considered, including negotiating complicated legal and regulatory frameworks as well as undertaking rigorous due diligence and property research. Throughout this book, we'll provide you practical insights, methods, and best practices to assist you overcome these obstacles. And best practices to guide you through these problems and make sound investment decisions.

Whether you are a seasoned investor trying to diversify your portfolio or a newbie to real estate investment, this book will provide you with the knowledge, skills, and confidence you need to succeed in the competitive world of commercial real estate. So, let's get started and learn about the wealth-building potential that commercial property investing has to offer!

Why Invest in Commercial Real Estate?

Commercial real estate investment has long been seen as a profitable way to accumulate wealth, generate passive income, and diversify investment portfolios. Commercial assets range from office buildings and retail centers to industrial warehouses and multifamily complexes, providing investors with a diverse variety of prospects for consistent profits and long-term development potential.

There are numerous compelling reasons for investors to commit resources to commercial real estate:

Revenue Generation: One of the most appealing aspects of commercial real estate is its capacity to produce steady rental revenue. Unlike residential properties, which typically yield lower rental returns, commercial properties command higher rental rates, providing investors with a consistent cash flow. Whether it's leasing office space to corporate tenants or renting retail storefronts to companies, commercial real estate investments have the potential for high rental yields.

Portfolio Diversification: Commercial real estate allows investors to expand their investment portfolios beyond traditional asset classes like equities and bonds. By including commercial properties in their investment portfolio, investors can lower total portfolio risk while increasing long-term profits. Commercial real estate has historically had little correlation with other asset classes, making it a good hedge against market volatility and economic downturns.

Appreciation Potential: In addition to rental income, commercial buildings can increase in value over time. As demand for commercial space grows owing to population growth, urbanization, and economic expansion, the value of commercial assets tends to rise,leading to capital appreciation for investors. Furthermore, investors may actively increase the value of their commercial properties by doing smart repairs, improvements, and repositioning activities, hence increasing appreciation potential.

Tax Advantages: Commercial real estate investments include many tax breaks that can help investors enhance their post-tax earnings. For example, investors may be able to deduct expenses such as property taxes, mortgage interest, depreciation, and maintenance costs, reducing their taxable income and lowering their overall tax obligation.

Commercial real estate owners may also profit from tax-deferred exchange alternatives, such as 1031 exchanges, which allow them to delay capital gains taxes by selling one property and reinvesting the proceeds in another like-kind property.

Inflation Hedge: Commercial real estate has historically been an efficient inflation hedge. As inflation rates rise, the value of physical assets like real estate rises, providing investors with a hedge against the declining purchase power of fiat currency. Furthermore, commercial property contracts sometimes have built-in rent escalations based on inflation indices, allowing investors to maintain the true worth of their rental revenue over time.

Control and Flexibility: Commercial real estate investments, unlike equities and mutual funds, provide investors with more control and flexibility. Investors have the authority to make strategic decisions about property purchase, financing, leasing, and management, allowing them to adapt their investment strategy to their individual aims and preferences.

Furthermore, commercial real estate investments can be organized in a variety of ways, including direct ownership, joint ventures, and real estate investment trusts (REITs), giving investors greater flexibility in their investment strategy.

Investing in commercial real estate has several advantages, including income creation, portfolio diversification, appreciation potential, tax breaks, inflation protection, and control over investment decisions. Commercial real estate offers an appealing opportunity for investors seeking consistent returns, long-term growth, and wealth preservation.

Chapter 1

Definition of a Commercial Investor

Understanding the function and qualities of a commercial investor is critical in real estate investment because it allows you to navigate the complicated terrain of commercial properties.

This digs into the concept of a commercial investor, examining the main characteristics, motives, and methods that set them apart from other investors.

To understand the job of a commercial investor, first define commercial real estate. Commercial real estate includes a wide range of property types utilized for commercial purposes, such as office buildings, retail centers, industrial warehouses, multifamily apartments, hotels, and mixed-use complexes.

In contrast to residential buildings, which are primarily utilized for habitation, commercial properties are leased or rented out to Businesses, renters, or investors who can create money.

A commercial investor is an individual or corporation who acquires, owns, manages, and operates commercial real estate assets to generate rental income or capital appreciation.

Commercial investors often have distinct features and characteristics that distinguish them from other sorts of investors, such as:

Sophisticated awareness: Commercial investors possess a thorough awareness of the commercial real estate sector, including property kinds, market trends, financial analysis, and investment methods. They have the knowledge and skills to find profitable investment possibilities and successfully manage risks.

Long-Term Vision: Commercial investors frequently have a long-term investment perspective, with the goal of growing wealth and providing consistent revenue streams over time. They value consistent cash flow, capital preservation, and wealth growth above short-term speculation or fast profits.

Commercial investors have a higher risk tolerance than other investors, as commercial real estate investments can be more complicated, volatile, and capital intensive. They are willing to take calculated risks and suffer market changes in order to maximize profits and diversify their portfolio.

Financial Resources: Commercial investors often have access to substantial financial resources, such as capital reserves, financing choices, and investment groups.
  They can use their financial resources to purchase, develop, or reposition commercial properties, as well as take advantage of market investment possibilities.

Commercial investors use strategic investing tactics that are adapted to their own aims, tastes, and market conditions.
They do extensive due diligence, market research, and financial analysis to find properties with high revenue, growth potential, and value-add opportunities.

Commercial investors have several reasons and purposes, including:

Revenue Generation: Commercial investors want to produce consistent rental revenue from their properties, which may act as a steady source of cash flow and passive income.

Capital Appreciation: Commercial investors seek capital appreciation by investing in properties that have the potential for value appreciation over time, which is influenced by market demand, property renovations, and economic growth.

Commercial investors diversify their investment portfolios by allocating funds to commercial properties and real estate assets, which have low correlation with traditional asset classes such as stocks and bonds, providing a hedge against market volatility.

Wealth Preservation: Commercial investors prioritize capital preservation and wealth accumulation, aiming to safeguard their assets and preserve their purchasing power against inflation and economic uncertainty.

Types of Commercial Property

Commercial real estate includes a wide range of property types, each having a unique commercial function and catering to a variety of companies and renters.

Understanding the many sorts of commercial properties is critical for investors, developers, and real estate professionals who want to navigate the commercial real estate market successfully.

In this part, we will look at and describe some of the most prevalent types of commercial properties:

Office Building

Office buildings are commercial facilities utilized for business operations such corporate offices, professional services, and administration. They range from single-tenant buildings to multi-tenant skyscrapers and are designated as Class A, B, or C depending on location, age, amenities, and rental costs.

Retail center

Retail centers are commercial properties that house retail enterprises, such as shopping malls, strip malls, power centers, and lifestyle centers. They include a variety of retail establishments, restaurants, entertainment venues, and other consumer-oriented companies that serve local communities and customer demand.

Industrial warehouse

Industrial warehouses are commercial assets that support manufacturing, distribution, storage, and logistical operations. They include warehouses, distribution centers, manufacturing plants, and flexible spaces that serve a variety of businesses, including e-commerce, logistics, manufacturing, and transportation.

Multifamily apartments

Multifamily apartments refer to residential properties having numerous housing units, including apartment buildings, condominiums, townhouses, and mixed-use complexes.

While largely residential in nature, multi-family homes are classified as commercial real estate when utilized for investment purposes and producing rental revenue from tenants.

Hotels and Hospitality Properties:

Hotels and hospitality properties offer housing, accommodation, and hospitality services to visitors and guests. They include full-service hotels, limited-service hotels, resorts, motels, boutique hotels, and bed-and-breakfasts that cater to both leisure and business tourists.

Medical and Healthcare Facilities:

Medical and healthcare facilities are commercial assets that offer healthcare services, such as hospitals, medical office buildings, outpatient clinics, urgent care centers, and specialist treatment centers. They serve patients' medical requirements and frequently house medical practitioners, healthcare professionals, and medical equipment.

Mixed-Use Developments:

Mixed-use projects are commercial properties with several purposes, including residential, retail, office, and entertainment. They develop lively, walkable communities with a varied range of facilities, services, and activities for residents, workers, and tourists alike.

Each form of commercial property has distinct characteristics, investment concerns, and market dynamics that investors must consider when assessing investment prospects.

Commercial real estate investments' performance and profitability are heavily influenced by factors such as location, tenant mix, market demand, and economic trends.

By being acquainted with the various types of commercial properties, investors may make educated decisions and capitalize on possibilities in the dynamic commercial real estate market.

Chapter 2

Understanding Commercial Real Estate Investing

We set out to investigate the foundations of investing in commercial real estate, giving readers a thorough grasp of the main ideas, approaches, and factors that go into this exciting and lucrative avenue for saving money.

Understanding Commercial Real Estate investment: The goal of commercial real estate investment is to acquire, own, lease, and manage properties that generate revenue in order to either increase in value through capital gains or rental income.

Commercial assets include office space, retail establishments, industrial facilities, and multifamily residences. Generally, these are utilized for commercial reasons.

Commercial real estate covers a wider range of property types and investment techniques than residential real estate, which is primarily focused on dwelling holdings.

Advantages of Investing in Commercial Real Estate:

Investing in commercial real estate has several advantages, which add to its allure for investors. One of the main advantages is stable cash flow, since long-term tenant leases on commercial buildings frequently result in steady rental revenue.

Commercial real estate also has the ability to increase in value over time due to a variety of variables, including economic expansion, property upgrades, and market demand. Another benefit is portfolio diversification, as commercial real estate has little connection to more conventional assets and can act as a buffer against market volatility for investors. Moreover, tax benefits associated with commercial real estate investments, such as tax-deferred exchanges, mortgage interest deductions, and depreciation deductions, can improve total profits.

Finally, because of their higher rents and property values, commercial buildings act as an inflation hedge.

Risk and Challenges:

Investing in commercial real estate has a number of dangers and difficulties in spite of the possible gains. Economic downturns can affect rental revenue and occupancy rates, which can result in losses for investors.

Another issue is the possibility of unoccupied premises leading to lower rental income and higher running costs.

Investors also need to take into account property-specific risks like environmental dangers or structural difficulties, as well as tenant defaults and capital market volatility.

Preserving wealth and attaining long-term investing success need an understanding of and commitment to managing these risks.

Factors Affecting the Commercial Real Estate Market:

A wide range of factors, including economic indicators like GDP growth, employment rates, and consumer spending, affect the commercial real estate market.

The market demand for commercial properties is significantly shaped by demographic changes, including population growth, migration patterns, and aging demographics.

The dynamics of supply and demand, interest rates, and governmental rules like construction requirements and zoning laws all have an influence on the commercial real estate market. To spot new trends and seize investing opportunities, investors need to keep a careful eye on certain market dynamics.

Investment Strategies and Methods: To meet their investment goals, commercial real estate investors use a variety of investment strategies and methods. Value-add strategies concentrate on increasing the value of failing buildings through repairs, repositioning, or redevelopment, whereas buy-and-hold strategies purchase assets with steady cash flow and long-term appreciation potential.

While development plans entail building from the ground up or redeveloping existing properties, opportunistic strategies target distressed or undervalued assets with strong upside potential.

Every strategy has a unique risk-return profile and needs to be carefully planned, carried out, and managed in order to be successful.

Investors may increase their chances of success and meet their financial objectives by making well-informed judgments and navigating the market with skill when it comes to commercial real estate investing. Regardless of experience level or lack thereof, this offers insightful advice and direction to assist you confidently and clearly manage the difficulties of investing in commercial real estate.

Chapter 3

An Intensive Course on Investing in Commercial Real Estate

"A Crash Course in Commercial Real Estate Investing" gives readers a concise yet thorough rundown of the essential ideas, tactics, and factors to take into account before entering the commercial real estate market. For first-time investors who want to learn the basics of investing in commercial real estate and make wise choices, this section acts as a primer.

Recognizing the Fundamentals:

The crash course starts out by exposing readers to the fundamentals of investing in commercial real estate, such as what constitutes a commercial property, the kinds of properties that are on the market, and the role that investors play in purchasing and overseeing these properties. It covers key ideas including regularly utilized financing choices, costs, rental revenue, and property assessment.

Market Dynamics and Trends:

The crash course then delves into the supply and demand dynamics, economic indicators, demographic trends, and market cycles that are influencing the commercial real estate market. It emphasizes how crucial it is to carry out in-depth market research and analysis in order to spot new possibilities, evaluate market risks, and make wise investment choices.

Investment tactics and techniques:

The crash course gives a general understanding of the several techniques and tactics that investors in commercial real estate use, including development, buy-and-hold, value-add, and opportunistic strategies. It outlines the fundamental ideas and factors for every strategy, such as investment timeframes, risk-return profiles, and exit tactics.

Due Diligence and Risk Management:

Performing due diligence and risk management is a crucial part of investing in commercial real estate. The crash course places a strong emphasis on the value of doing extensive due diligence on real estate, which includes financial analysis, market research, legal examination, and physical inspections. Additionally, it covers risk management techniques like insurance, contingency planning, and diversification that help to reduce possible hazards and protect investors' cash.

Capital Structures and Financing:

Complex capital structures and financing are frequently involved in commercial real estate transactions. An overview of the common financing methods accessible to investors in commercial real estate is given in the crash course. These choices include private equity, syndication, conventional bank loans, and commercial mortgages. It helps investors properly traverse the financing process by outlining the important terms, structures, and factors related to each financing choice.

Legal and Regulatory Considerations:

Navigating the legal and regulatory landscape is essential in commercial real estate investing. The crash course highlights the legal and regulatory considerations involved in commercial real estate transactions, such as zoning laws, building codes, environmental regulations, lease agreements, and property taxes. It emphasizes the importance of seeking legal counsel and conducting thorough legal due diligence to ensure compliance with applicable laws and regulations.

Commercial Real Estate

Chapter 4

Getting Investment Leads for Commercial Property

Identifying and locating possible investment prospects in the commercial real estate market is a critical part of the investing process, and here is where getting leads on commercial property investment comes in. This section looks at several approaches and techniques for finding leads on commercial real estate, which may help investors find profitable ventures and take advantage of market trends.

Market research and analysis:

Conducting market research and analysis is one of the main techniques to obtain leads for investing in commercial real estate. To find markets and submarkets with high demand for commercial properties, investors might use market data, demographic trends, economic indicators, and property listings.

Through the examination of key market factors like rental growth, vacancy rates, and supply-demand dynamics, investors may identify places that have advantageous investment circumstances and focus their search appropriately.

Networking and Relationship Building

Within the commercial real estate industry, networking and relationship building may be extremely helpful in locating potential investment opportunities.

Investors can network with brokers, agents, developers, property owners, and other industry experts who could have access to off-market bargains or unique opportunities by attending industry events, networking gatherings, and real estate conferences.

Building connections with professionals and market specialists in the area may give investors access to possible investments, insightful advice, and recommendations.

Real Estate Agents and Brokers

Interacting with brokers and agents that specialize in commercial real estate is another good approach to obtain leads on possible investments.

These experts have access to unique properties, off-market transactions, and market listings that might not be easily found by the general public. Investors may utilize the networks and knowledge of seasoned commercial real estate brokers to find possibilities that meet their investment goals by sharing their investment criteria and objectives with them.

Online Platforms and markets

Investors may access a variety of property listings, investment possibilities, and market data through online platforms and markets devoted to commercial real estate.

Using websites like Crexi, CoStar, and LoopNet, investors may look for commercial properties based on the investment targets, size, kind, and location of the property.

These platforms frequently provide thorough property listings with complete descriptions, financial data, and listing agents' contact information. This helps investors perform preliminary research and due diligence on possible investment possibilities.

Direct Marketing and Outreach

Through proactive outreach and direct marketing initiatives, investors may also provide leads. To find out more about off-market prospects or distressed properties, this may entail cold phoning developers, property owners, and prospective sellers as well as sending targeted mailings and email campaigns.

Investors can draw in property owners wishing to sell or divest their commercial properties and start conversations about possible investments by clearly outlining their investment requirements, financial capacity, and desire to deal.

Investment Groups and Syndicates

Investing in commercial real estate through investment groups, syndicates, or real estate investment trusts (REITs) may give investors access to institutional-grade assets, diversified portfolios, and pooled money.

These investment entities frequently have pre-existing networks, pipelines for deals, and investment strategies that are concentrated on buying and overseeing commercial real estate.

By taking part in these organizations, investors may access investment possibilities that would be beyond their individual grasp by utilizing the collective knowledge, resources, and transaction flow.

Obtaining leads for investing in commercial real estate necessitates a proactive, multifaceted strategy that includes focused outreach, networking, market research, and teamwork. In the dynamic and cutthroat commercial real estate market, investors may find profitable investment opportunities, create a strong investment pipeline, and eventually reach their financial objectives by utilizing a variety of tactics and approaches.

Chapter 5

Commercial Deal Negotiation and Closure

Commercial real estate deal negotiation and completion is a complex process with many parties involved, complex negotiations, and close attention to detail. We dig more deeply into the subtleties of due diligence concerns, negotiating tactics, and the necessary procedures for concluding commercial real estate deals in this chapter.

Comprehending the Process of Negotiation

In commercial real estate negotiations, parties work to balance their interests, preferences, and goals in order to get to a mutually agreeable settlement through a dynamic and iterative process. A successful negotiation goes through numerous phases, such as:

Before entering into a negotiation, it is essential that you plan well. This entails investigating the state of the market, evaluating similar homes, figuring out the seller's intentions, and setting precise goals for the negotiation.

Communication

Clear expectations, informational exchanges, and problem-solving all depend on effective communication. Constructive negotiations are facilitated by open and honest communication since it develops rapport and trust between the parties.

Negotiation Dynamics

Power, leverage, and reciprocity are frequently balanced delicately in negotiations. Competent negotiators use their comprehension of these dynamics to promote their interests while respecting the opposing party's goals and concerns. They also shape talks and impact perceptions.

In order to break deadlocks and come to mutually agreeable agreements, parties need to be able to explore other solutions, trade-offs, and concessions. This is where flexibility and creativity come into play.

Resolution of disputes

Sustaining the integrity of negotiations and keeping relationships requires the constructive handling of disputes and disagreements. Effective conflict resolution strategies include compromise, active listening, and empathy. These strategies aid in lowering tensions and assisting parties in reaching an understanding.

Handling the Process of Due Diligence

During the crucial due diligence phase of a commercial real estate deal, purchasers thoroughly investigate the property to evaluate its potential, hazards, and appropriateness. Important things to think about when doing due diligence are:

Property Inspection

Performing comprehensive physical examinations to evaluate the state of the property, spot any neglected upkeep or structural problems, and calculate the price of repairs and renovations.

Examining financial records, such as revenue statements, rent rolls, operational costs, and capital expenditures, in order to assess the property's cash flow and overall financial performance

Legal & Regulatory conformity

To guarantee adherence to relevant rules and reduce potential liabilities, confirming the property's conformity with building codes, zoning laws, environmental laws, and other legal requirements.

Tenant Analysis

Analyzing leases, occupancy rates, lease expiry dates, and tenant creditworthiness to determine the leasing profile, possibility for revenue stability, and prospective for tenant retention of the property.

Essential Facts to Take Into Account When Sealing Commercial Deals

Finalizing the sale and giving the buyer possession of the property are the two main components of closing a commercial real estate deal. In the closing process, important factors to take into account are:

Executing legal Documents

Signing and completing various legal documents that have been produced by escrow agents or attorneys, such as the purchase agreement, deed, and closing statement.

Funding and Financing

Obtaining the acquisition funded, which includes securing mortgage loans, setting up financing conditions, and making sure there is enough cash on hand to cover the down payment and closing charges.

Ownership Examination and Insurance

Finding ownership rights through a title examination and getting title insurance to guard against unanticipated title flaws or claims that could surface after closing.

Closing monies and Escrow

Before closing, make sure all parties meet their individual responsibilities and terms stated in the purchase agreement by depositing closing monies into an escrow account.

Title Transfer and Recording

To formally transfer ownership of the property from the seller to the buyer, the deed and other legal papers must be recorded with the relevant government agencies.

Deals involving commercial real estate involve ability, patience, and meticulous attention to detail. Investors may accomplish their financial goals and successfully close commercial real estate deals by grasping the negotiating process, doing careful due diligence, and managing the closing procedure.

Commercial Real Estate

Chapter 6

Overseeing and Regulating Business Real Estate

To preserve asset value, maximize revenues, and guarantee tenant happiness, commercial buildings must be properly managed and maintained. Here, we look at how to maximize the performance and lifespan of commercial real estate investments via the study of best practices in property management, tenant relations, lease agreements, and maintenance plans.

Top Property Management Techniques

Managing a commercial property's finances, tenant relations, upkeep, and compliance are just a few of the many facets that need to be thoroughly reviewed in order to achieve effective property management. Important recommendations for property management encompass:

Financial Management:

Enforcing strict financial management procedures to guarantee the property stays within its allocated budget and has a positive cash flow. These procedures include budgeting, rent collecting, spending tracking, and financial reporting.

Tenant Selection and Screening

Choosing renters who meet the goals and leasing requirements of the property requires extensive tenant screening procedures to evaluate applicants' appropriateness, creditworthiness, and leasing history.

Effectively managing lease agreements, including negotiations, renewals, rent adjustments, and lease compliance monitoring, is necessary to guarantee that renters follow the terms of the lease and carry out their end of the bargain.

Property Inspections and Maintenance

To preserve property value and tenant satisfaction, do routine property inspections and maintenance checks to find maintenance issues, safety risks, and compliance concerns. Then, swiftly resolve them.

Risk Management and Compliance

Keeping up with local, state, and federal rules, obtaining enough insurance coverage, and putting risk management procedures into place to safeguard the property and its inhabitants are all ways to mitigate risk and ensure regulatory compliance.

Important factors for lease agreements and tenant relations

Effective Communication

To promote trust and openness, keep lines of communication open with renters, immediately resolve their complaints, and provide timely updates on property-related topics.

Lease negotiation

Creating fair and acceptable conditions, rental prices, lease incentives, and opportunities for renewal in order to draw and keep great renters. Balancing the interests of landlords and tenants.

Tenant Services and Amenities

To improve tenant satisfaction and foster a pleasant renter experience, provide tenants with services and amenities including maintenance support, security services, common area upkeep, and recreational facilities.

Lease enforcement is the process of upholding lease agreements and protecting landlord rights by enforcing terms and conditions consistently, responding quickly to noncompliance, and pursuing appropriate legal action as needed.

Tenant Retention tactics

To foster long-term tenant relationships and reduce tenant turnover, tenant retention tactics such as proactive communication, responsive property management, lease renewal incentives, and tenant appreciation events should be put into practice.

Strategies for Upkeep and Maintenance

Proactive planning, consistent upkeep, and prompt repairs are necessary for commercial property care in order to protect asset value and guarantee tenant happiness. Important upkeep and maintenance techniques consist of:

Preventive maintenance includes periodic building assessments, HVAC system inspections, roof inspections, plumbing checks, and other proactive maintenance programs that are put into place to find and fix possible problems before they become serious.

Scheduled Inspections

Regular property inspections to evaluate the state of the facility, pinpoint maintenance requirements, and quickly resolve any safety risks, code infractions, or compliance problems.

Vendor management is the process of choosing trustworthy suppliers, contractors, and service providers for upkeep and repairs, negotiating advantageous contracts, and monitoring vendor performance to guarantee high-caliber output and economical fixes.

Emergency Response Planning

Ensuring the safety and protection of tenants' property while creating extensive emergency response plans and processes to handle unanticipated situations, such as fire crises, natural catastrophes, or security problems.

Capital Improvement Projects

To increase property value, draw in tenants, and keep a competitive edge in the market, planning and carrying out capital improvement projects, such as building renovations, upgrades, or energy efficiency increases, is essential.

A planned and proactive strategy that includes financial management, tenant relations, lease administration, and maintenance methods is necessary for the efficient management and upkeep of commercial facilities. Landlords may maximize property performance, reduce risk, and succeed over the long term in the commercial real estate market by putting best practices into effect, cultivating excellent tenant relationships, and placing a high priority on property care.

Risk mitigation and Return Optimization

Reducing risks and increasing returns are critical goals for investors looking to maximize their investment portfolios in the ever-changing world of commercial real estate investing. To achieve long-term investing success in commercial real estate, this chapter explores key techniques for risk management, diversification, portfolio management, and increasing property value.

Techniques for Risk Management

Identifying, evaluating, and reducing the risks that might affect the profitability of an investment is a crucial part of commercial real estate investing.

Strategies for risk management that work well include:

Exercise Due Diligence

To evaluate investment prospects and examine property fundamentals, market dynamics, and potential dangers, a thorough due diligence process is required. Performing thorough financial analyses, legal evaluations, and property inspections assists in identifying and reducing possible hazards before entering into a transaction.

Risk Assessment

Identifying and evaluating a wide range of risks, including financial, operational, market, and regulatory risks, is necessary when conducting a thorough risk assessment. Investors may create risk mitigation strategies that are suited to their individual investment goals and risk tolerance levels by having a thorough understanding of the nature and extent of hazards.

Implementing risk mitigation strategies can assist lower exposure to possible hazards and lessen their influence on investment performance.
Examples of these strategies include diversification, insurance coverage, contingency planning, and contractual safeguards. Investors may spread risk and improve portfolio resilience by diversifying their holdings among a range of property types, geographies, and asset classes.

Monitoring and Adaptation

Investors can detect new hazards and modify their investment plans by keeping a close eye on macroeconomic variables, property performance, and market circumstances. . By staying informed and proactive, investors can mitigate risks effectively and seize opportunities to optimize investment returns.

Commercial Real Estate

Chapter 7

The Management of Portfolios and Diversification

A key component of portfolio management is diversification, which is allocating investment funds among a range of assets in order to lower total risk and improve long-term returns.

Important facets of portfolio management and diversification

Asset Allocation

Based on investment goals, risk tolerance, and time horizon, strategic asset allocation identifies the best combination of asset classes, including stocks, bonds, real estate, and alternative assets. Capital is distributed among several asset classes to assist an investment portfolio's risk and return potential be balanced.

Property diversification reduces concentration risk and exposure to certain market dynamics by spreading real estate investments over a variety of property types, industries, and geographical areas. The stability and resilience of a portfolio to market swings may be improved by investing in a diverse portfolio of assets, which should include office buildings, retail centers, industrial warehouses, residential properties, and mixed-use developments.

Periodic portfolio rebalancing entails modifying asset allocations to preserve targeted risk-return profiles and match investment plans with evolving market circumstances. Rebalancing is a strategy used to reduce excessive risk exposure and maximize portfolio performance. It may entail shifting cash across particular properties, sectors, or asset classes.

Risk Management instrument

During market downturns or turbulent times, investors may protect themselves from downside risk and preserve wealth by using risk management instruments including derivatives, options, and hedging methods.

Using risk management techniques improves risk-adjusted returns and protects investment money from unanticipated occurrences when combined with a diversified portfolio approach.

Techniques to Raise the Value of Your Property

For investors in commercial real estate who want to maximize profits and improve asset performance, increasing property value is a core goal. Important techniques to raise the value of a property include:

Capital improvements

Investing in projects that will improve a property's functionality, appearance, and marketability can raise the property's value and potential rental income. Examples of these projects include building renovations, tenant improvements, energy efficiency upgrades, and technological advancements.

Repositioning assets through smart rebranding, repositioning, and redevelopment projects can uncover latent value and draw in better tenants, which will raise occupancy, rental rates, and property appreciation. This process is known as asset repositioning.

Operational Efficiency

Putting into practice strategies for cost-saving, operational streamlining, and expenditure management may optimize property performance and enhance net operating income (NOI), which improves overall worth of real estate and financial gains.

Success Stories and Real-Life Case Studies

We examine real-world case studies and investment success stories involving commercial real estate, providing insightful analysis, important lessons, and critical takeaways for investors hoping to replicate success in their own ventures.

Case Studies of Profitable Investments in Commercial Real Estate:

Redevelopment of Office Buildings

One noteworthy case study focuses on the effective conversion of an outdated office building into a contemporary Class-A workspace. Numerous changes were made as part of the redevelopment, including updates to the interior and tenant amenities as well as front enhancements.

The property's value and investment returns significantly rose as a consequence of the rehabilitation activities, which also saw a rise in leasing activity, better rental rates, and enhanced tenant satisfaction.

Retail mall Repositioning

A further interesting case study focuses on how tenant mix optimization and deliberate rebranding helped turn around a failing retail mall.

The site was turned into a bustling hub for food, entertainment, and retail by bringing in well-known stores, adding anchor tenants, and improving the entire shopping experience.

Significant value creation and capital appreciation resulted from the effective repositioning activities, which also raised investor confidence, improved foot traffic, and occupancy rates.

Expansion of an Industrial Warehouse

The third case study describes the effective enlargement of an industrial warehouse to accommodate the increasing needs of logistics and e-commerce tenants.

Securing long-term leasing deals with significant e-commerce businesses, installing cutting-edge logistics infrastructure, and adding more space footage were all part of the expansion project.

The property was able to benefit from the growing e-commerce business, provide steady rental revenue, and see considerable asset appreciation over time thanks to the planned expansion.

Principal Learning Outcomes and Conclusions:

Planning and Strategic Vision

These case studies' success highlights the need of having a thorough planning process and a well-defined strategic vision. Market trends and investor demand are closely examined by savvy investors, who also create effective strategies and spot value-added possibilities.

The identification of value-add possibilities is a crucial aspect of commercial real estate investing in order to optimize profits. Investors may uncover latent value by boosting property functioning, upgrading tenant amenities, and maximizing income streams—whether through property repositioning, redevelopment, or expansion initiatives.

The Tenant-Centric Approach

Encouraging occupancy, retention, and long-term success requires putting the requirements of tenants first and attending to their demands. Great tenant experiences, solid tenant connections, and value-added services are the main priorities of successful investors to attract and retain high-quality tenants.

Flexibility and Adaptability

Because the commercial real estate market is dynamic and always changing, investors must continue to be flexible and adaptive in their investing approaches. Prosperous investors welcome change, adjust course as needed, and take advantage of market openings to maximize investment returns.

Last but not least, ongoing education and development are critical to long-term success in the commercial real estate market. In order to maximize investment returns and fulfill their financial goals, savvy investors maintain a proactive approach, keep up with market developments, and make use of industry best practices for their long-term financial goals.

Chapter 8

Your Next Moves in Investing in Commercial Real Estate

This chapter provides you with the information and direction you need to make informed decisions and succeed in commercial real estate investing, from developing your investment strategy to utilizing resources and tools for additional study.

Formulating Your Investment Strategy

Establish Your Investment Goals

To begin, establish your investment goals, which should include your time horizon, risk tolerance, and financial aspirations. You can make decisions and set clear guidelines for your investing plan by being clear about your goals.

Evaluate Your Risk Profile

To determine how much risk and uncertainty you can accept while making investments, do a thorough evaluation of your risk profile. When assessing risk tolerance levels, take into account elements like your financial resources, expertise with investments, and personal preferences.

Establish Investment criterion

Establish your criterion for investments based on your choices for target market groups, property types, and geographic locations as well as your expected returns. Your property search will go more smoothly if you have clear investing criteria in place, which will also guarantee that your objectives are met.

Create a Diversified Portfolio Strategy

Distribute funds among various property kinds, asset classes, and geographical areas to create a diversified portfolio strategy. Investment risk can be reduced, risk-adjusted returns can be maximized, portfolio resilience to market swings can be strengthened through diversification.

Establish an Actionable Investment Plan

Write out your goals for the investment, the properties you are targeting, the purchase and financing strategies, and the exit plans. To establish responsibility and measure progress, break down your strategy into manageable tasks and deadlines.

Further Reading Materials & Resources:
Learning Tools

To expand your understanding of the concepts, tactics, and best practices of commercial real estate investment, study through learning tools including books, webinars, online courses, and trade journals. To be knowledgeable and powerful as an investor, seek out reliable sources and professional opinions.

Opportunities for Networking

Meet people in the business, become a member of real estate investing organizations, go to networking functions, and interact with others in the field to broaden your professional network and gain access to opportunities, opportunities, and guidance from industry experts and seasoned investors.

Market Research Tools

Use data analytics platforms, real estate market reports, and market research tools to confidently assess investment possibilities, uncover new trends, and do in-depth market analysis.

Financial Modeling Software

To analyze risk-return profiles and investment viability, make cash flow estimates, analyze possible investments financially, and conduct scenario analysis, use financial modeling software and investment analysis tools.

Expert Counseling Services

To manage intricate investment deals, reduce risks, and maximize investment returns, think about consulting with licensed real estate specialists, such as brokers, lawyers, accountants, and financial counselors.

Supplementary Materials and Index

To help you learn more about commercial real estate investing, we've included an appendix with a carefully chosen selection of websites and other resources. You may also easily traverse the complex language used in the sector by using the extensive dictionary of words related to commercial real estate that is supplied.

Sites and Organizations Suggested

Web sites:

The Commercial Real Estate Development Association (NAIOP) offers experts in the field of commercial real estate insightful information, tools, and research.

The CCIM Institute provides certification courses and specialized instruction in financial modeling and commercial real estate investment analysis.

Urban Land Institute (ULI): Provides publications, events, and industry research on real estate investment and urban development.
Establishments:

The National Association of Realtors (NAR): is an organization that advocates for commercial real estate practitioners and represents real estate professionals.

The International Council of Shopping Centers (ICSC): provides professionals in the retail real estate sector with research, education, and networking opportunities.

The Institute of Real Estate Management (IREM): offers real estate professionals and property managers networking opportunities, certification, and education.

Glossary of Terms Used in Commercial Real Estate:

The capitalization rate, or cap rate, measures the rate of return on an investment property in real estate by comparing the income generated to the property's market value.

Net operating income (NOI) is the entire revenue from a property less operating costs; it does not include capital expenditures or debt repayment.

Cash-on-Cash Return: The proportion of a property's yearly pre-tax cash flow to the total amount of money invested in it.

The percentage of empty units or space in a rental property as a percentage of all available units or space is known as the vacancy rate.

Lease Term: The length of a lease, usually stated in years or months, that a landlord and renter agree upon.

Tenant Improvement (TI) Allowance: Money given to the tenant by the landlord to make upgrades or modifications to the rented premises.

Loan-to-worth (LTV) Ratio: The percentage relationship between the loan amount and the property's purchase price or appraised worth.

An exit strategy is a plan that describes how an investor plans to sell or liquidate an investment property in order to reduce losses or realize gains.

1031 Exchange: This is a type of tax-deferred exchange that lets investors postpone paying capital gains taxes by selling one property and using the profits to buy another like-kind property.

Due Diligence is the process of carrying out in-depth analyses and evaluations of the financial, legal, and physical aspects of a property prior to finalizing a deal.

The terminology often used in commercial real estate investing may be better understood and interpreted with the help of this glossary, which also offers insight into the nuances of the field.

Last Thought

It is crucial to consider the most important realizations and lessons discovered throughout this voyage through the world of commercial real estate investing. We've looked at the core ideas, tactics, and industry best practices that propel success in the exciting and lucrative world of commercial real estate throughout this book.

Fundamentally, investing in commercial real estate has unmatched chances for long-term financial development, portfolio diversification, and wealth generation. Investors may realize their financial goals and harness the enormous potential of commercial properties by utilizing market research, strategic planning, and careful execution.

As you go out on your own investment adventure in commercial real estate, keep in mind these important points:

Knowledge is Power, therefore keep learning about current market trends, smart investing techniques, and best practices in the business. To make wise investing selections, keep up with changing market conditions and new possibilities.

Managing Risk is Essential: Reduce the risk associated with investments by carrying out careful due diligence, evaluating the state of the market, and putting risk mitigation plans into practice. To reduce your exposure to market swings and guard against negative risks, diversify your investing portfolio.

Maintaining Calm and Effort Pay Off: Patience, determination, and a long-term outlook are necessary for success in commercial real estate investing. Even in the face of difficulty, be ready to weather market cycles, overcome obstacles, and maintain focus on your investing objectives.

Network and Work Together: Establish connections with business leaders, take advantage of networking events, and look for seasoned investors to serve as mentors. Work together with peers, advisers, and real estate experts to obtain knowledge, acquire access to resources, and broaden your network of potential investors.

Proactive, decisive, and action-oriented investors are the most successful ones. Apply the wisdom and understanding you've learned from this book to your future investing ventures. Gradually increase the size of your investing portfolio over time by starting small, but do so now.

To sum up, investing in commercial real estate is a dynamic and fulfilling path that offers several chances for development, achievement, and happiness. Through smart investments in commercial real estate, you may potentially reach your financial objectives, accumulate wealth, and add long-term value by putting the ideas and tactics in this book to use.

Always keep in mind that every choice you make about your investments is a chance for you to develop, learn, and hone your investing abilities. Continue to be inquisitive, be committed, and never give up on your goals of becoming financially independent and succeeding in the commercial real estate market.

Cheers to many more years of success and wealth in the fascinating field of commercial real estate!

www.ingramcontent.com/pod-product-compliance
Lightning Source LLC
Chambersburg PA
CBHW070413230526
45471CB00006B/2789